MW00581669

73

ADVANCED
TUBA
STUDIES

By JAROSLAV CIMERA

73 Advanced Tuba Etudes

JAROSLAV CIMERA

Play the first five scales in two speeds.

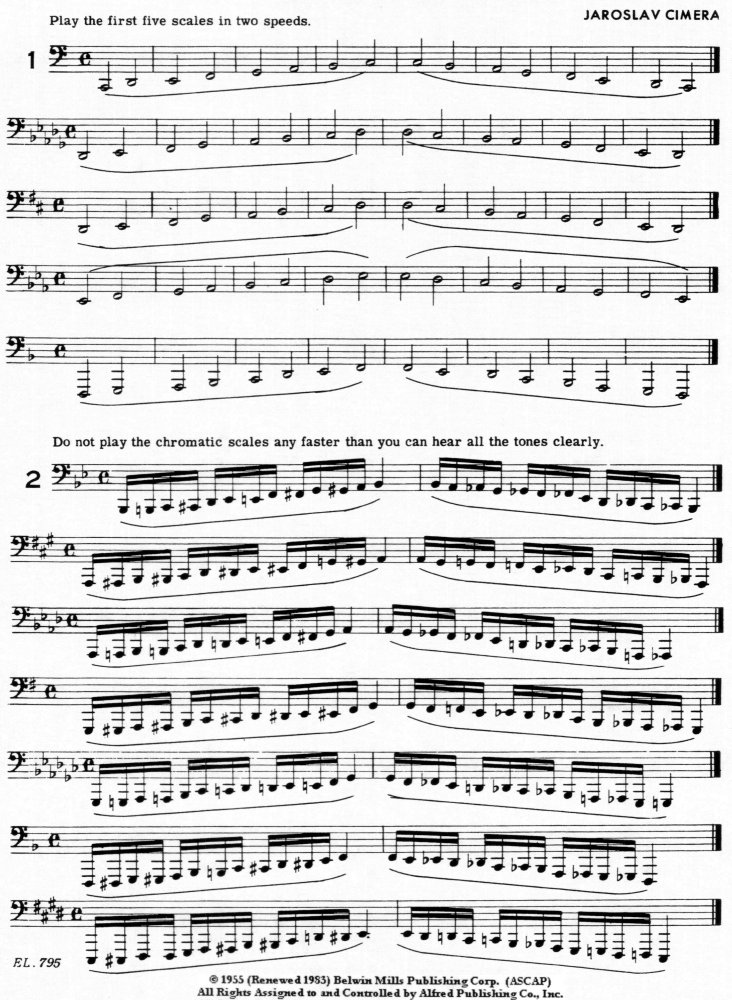

Do not play the chromatic scales any faster than you can hear all the tones clearly.

EL. 795

Major Scales

Play the following Scales in 3 speeds, as soft as possible, starting with half notes.
Play the 4th speed with full tone and as fast as possible.

Minor Scales

Minor Scales

Melodic Minor

Harmonic Minor

Melodic Minor

Harmonic Minor

Melodic Minor

Harmonic Minor

Melodic Minor

Harmonic Minor

Melodic Minor

Harmonic Minor

Melodic Minor

Harmonic Minor

6

EL. 795

7

EL.795

9

EL.795

10

EL. 795

Vivace

17

Allegro

18

12

EL. 795

14

EL.795

18

20

EL.795

22

EL.795

24

28

EL.795

30

EL.795